MW00939991

Copyright © :

ISBN: 9781705865828 (Paperback)

Library of Congress Control Number: 00000000000

Any references to historical events, real people, or real places are used fictitiously. Names, characters, and places are products of the author's imagination. .

Cover design by Deziner Zone found at www.DesignCrowd.com
Pictures from Pexels.com
Printed by Kindle Direct Publishing, in the United States of America.
Developmental Editing by Greg Brown.
https://reedsy.com/greg-brown

First printing edition 2019.

Tensen Group LLC
www.tensengroup.com

The Part Time Start-up: Building a business while working full time

Acknowledgements

The Part-time Startup:

Building a Business
While Working Full-time

Contents

Acknowledgements

Acknowledgements

There are so many people I'd like to thank for helping me with this book. The list is incredibly long. So many people have helped me along the way and helped guide me to where I am today. Special thanks to Kate, who encourages me to be better every day, and who encouraged me to start writing this book. She saw the passion I have in teaching and giving back and she urged me to keep pursuing it and ultimately write about it.

Also, I want to thank the many folks I work with. Believe it or not, the bad days at work drive me to do more outside of work. So, with some irony, I am thanking the folks who made my work difficult. If it was always easy, and I always felt successful, I would never have started a business, nor would I have started this book.

Acknowledgements

Forward

The goal of this book is to guide you on your way to determining what you want and what kind of business you want to create.

If you are looking to start the next Google, the next Facebook, or some other similar company, you probably won't gain a ton of value from this book. What you might find, however, is a way to grow a business that allows you to make the decision of when, or if you quit your job, enabling you to build a better life.

Forward

As you read, you might start wondering what drove me to write this. Well, when you hate your boss, but the job pays well, you feel like you don't have control. Ever been there? I know I have. (O, and in case my current boss is reading this -- for the record, my current bosses are amazing)

Eventually, you get to the point where you have to find a way to gain control of your life. Enter this book. With some luck, you will find a way to feel free from a bad boss, and free to walk away if you ever need to – without worrying about where your next paycheck is coming from. If all goes well, you'll become your own boss and your own income generator. Some people call this making sure you have your "F you" money. I view this as a way to free yourself, but more importantly, to keep your soul alive for those days when you hate what you do. They have happened to all of us, after all.

There is something else about this book that you should know. It is much more about you, then about a startup. While you might feel that this book title is a bit misleading, having consulted for many start up companies, it isn't the idea that fails a startup. It's the person. Yes – YOU. You will be the reason any start up business you create is successful or fails. That is why much of this book focus' on your development before we ever touch the key foundational aspects to consider when you are choosing and building your company.

PART I – The Part-Time Startup:

Building Your Business

The Beginning

What am I passionate about? That was the question I kept returning to when I first started thinking about writing.

I thought about what I often ended up coaching and mentoring on, and I thought about my own accomplishments. When you've managed to earn as much outside of an impressive career as you have within that career, you realize that maybe that is a topic that people want to learn about! Maybe about how you've managed to build a business that can allow you to walk away from any job, and still feel financially unconcerned – all done by the time you were 30.

I realized I've been successful at ensuring that when I work for a company, they're not my only source of income. As a result, I've had the freedom to make decisions and take actions without having to fear what my bosses think or, worst case, without the fear of potentially losing my job. This freedom is empowering. It lets me think clearly, strategically, and fearlessly.

One of the things you'll be thinking about when you start reading this book is making more money. That's one reason to read, and, of course, a pretty good one. Learning how to balance building a business while maintaining the safety and security of your career is another reason.

Personally, one thing I always want to prevent is growing fearful of getting fired from my job - of losing that stream of income.

That source of income represents a sense of security and peace of mind. My goal is that you, the reader, will walk away feeling that you have the ability to take ownership, take control, and make sure that you walk away truly in control of your destiny.

This is a book designed for people to really understand how important their choices are, in everything they do. When we think about what's going to make us successful, every choice we make has the potential to make or break that success.

Furthermore, it's crucial to recognize that while choice is important, both action and non-action are equally critical. Do your actions and the choices you make stem from a true understanding of what

PART I – The Part-Time Startup:
Building Your Business

decisions you are making? What planning did you put in place? What did you do for pre-work? What did you come prepared for? These are questions we'll learn to continually ask. Let's take a page out of the book "The Art of War" – the victorious warriors win first, then they go to war.

In this book, we're going to go through a whole bunch of different topics. At the end of the day, you'll likely love it or hate it. For my sake, if you hate it, I hope that it still occasionally makes you laugh. As we go through the chapters, you might find yourself grinning and thinking, *Huh, this book is the greatest thing since sliced bread*. Yes, I put a picture of Sliced Bread.

Maybe you'll laugh. More than likely, you might find yourself saying, "Holy shit, that arrogant prick is clearly from the northeast and doesn't get anything or anyone outside himself or his circle. I wasted money on this?" Okay, so perhaps that's an extreme reaction. But I believe in covering all possibilities. Jokes can only do so much work after all. My hope is that you'll both like and learn from this reading experience. Let's start from the beginning.

PART I – The Part-Time Startup:
Building Your Business

Writing This Book

Chapter One, how to write a book! Okay, I'm kidding – kind of. Way back, when I was thinking about what my first chapter should be, I actually outlined the entire chapter, and then the entire book. Since then, it's changed about 1,000 times. The lesson: sometimes you don't really know the way until you're on the actual journey. That is true whether it's writing or figuring out how to build your life and career around a part-time startup. You are looking to find the road to more financial freedom, and the journey is applicable to all aspects of your life. Why do I bring this up? I started with a plan and adjusted it along the way when something new came along. If there is one constant you can be sure of, it's that things change.

But here's something I thought was kind of funny. Think of it as a writer's knock-knock joke, if you will.

Question: Hey, you know how you start writing a book?

Answer: You start writing!

I had *no idea*. It turned out that all the planning and outlining in the world wouldn't actually write a book. But without all that planning and outlining, I never would have gotten to the stage of actually writing.

First lesson: you've got to plan for a thing in order to get to the thing.

Why do you plan? What do you plan? How do you plan? Everything about this book is going to be on planning and choice. The choice of any writer is to write or not to write. For me, I wrote. With a plan. And oh my gosh writing went so much faster! At first, I planned to write a page per night, but because I kept failing to meet that goal, I adjusted. "How about I write 1,000 words a week?" I told myself. That's reasonable, right?

PART I – The Part-Time Startup:
Building Your Business

Then, when I started failing at that, I was like, "Okay, what do I need to do to change and motivate myself to actually write?" I realized that, while on a plane, if faced with the choice of writing or watching a movie, I chose to write! By learning about myself and my behavioral patterns I figured out a place where writing, for me at least, wasn't hard. Then I started to execute my vision.

When you realize that you keep failing at your goal, it isn't about 'trying harder' – my least favorite phrase. It also isn't about 'doing better' either! For the record, 'do better' is like nails on a chalk board for me. 'Do Better' reminds me of when people ask what the definition of insanity is! – it's doing things over and over the same way. But don't worry, we will do it better this time – I swear it. It will be the same, but it will be done better.

What we are trying to do – is look at yourself, and think differently. If you can't see a different way of doing things, maybe you need to try something radical and outside of the box, like walking on your hands. Or use a lifeline and phone a friend.

Side note: If Dakota Krout is reading this (for those who don't know, he's right now one of my favorite authors) – you somehow pump out a new book every three months. What the hell!? – "try hard" much?

Definition: Try Hard: What kids these days say to make fun of the nerds and dweebs out there. I am one.

Writing this book, focused on exploring things that make you successful. Because this is my first book, I really thought it would be fun to start with what it takes to write a book – in case any of you decide to follow in my footsteps.

(1) You determine the goal of the book.

      a. The goal of this book specifically is to provide you with insight into the value of choice, the value of taking control of your own life, and the foundations and steps to take in building your business, among other things!

(2) You start writing

(3) You edit and revise

(4) You repeat

(5) You serve chilled alcohol

PART I – The Part-Time Startup: Building Your Business

As you can see, there are a few things I'm hoping you'll gain from this book, and I'm hoping it's going to be a little bit more valuable than some of those other self-help books out there.

The Goal, by Eliyahu M. Goldratt, is one of my favorite books to suggest reading. It's a great read to compliment your education, and I highly recommend you grab a copy and read it. It's essentially a crash course on two words: "make money."

If you walk away feeling like you know how to make a little bit more money, you will accomplish the goal of this book as well. So, we're going to have fun with it.

I realize we're bouncing around a bit here, and one of the goals of this book *was not* to make a reader feel like the walls were shifting all around him or her and he or she was trapped in the movie "Inception." But stay the course with me if you will.

I started to solve my writer's block by figuring out a different way of thinking about writing (my plane epiphany). Developing other ways of thinking is critical for actually reaching the goals of this book, so I want to take a moment to point out another book that might provide insight into different ways of thinking. *The Richest Man in Babylon* by George S. Clason, is a very short book I absolutely adore. It's one of the inspirations for how I started my company, and helps guide everything that I've been doing as far as the head of a startup seeking to secure additional income and security. Take a look.

PART I – The Part-Time Startup: Building Your Business

It's very short, think like 100 pages short, and yet filled with great lessons.

Lastly, learn and study good investment philosophies. Start with Warren Buffet, who suggests you should buy and hold. What that really means: plan, plan, plan; buy something that is truly an investment and hold onto it as its value grows.

Choosing Your Business and Business Model – the Part-Time Way

Fundamentally, when you're looking at what kind of part-time business to create, you have a few options.

1. A business that is always going to be part-time – sometimes referred to as a "side hustle."
2. A business that you are expecting to become your new full-time job (this may have stemmed from your initial side hustle).
3. A business that will secure your retirement with very little effort on your part.

For this author, the business I chose will secure my retirement very early, and allow me the option to leave my job with security and freedom if I so choose. The model I chose was to invest in leveraged loans and rental properties. The key contributors I look at are return on investment, as well as return on equity. The model could also have very easily fallen under the first bullet as well, except that when you outsource property management, you trade time for income. This allows me focus on the macro investments, while not worrying about a broken faucet in a unit. This allows a secure path to retirement with little effort on my part.

A side hustle can take a wide variety of forms. You can be a real estate agent during the evenings. You can be fulfilling orders and shipping out things as a small distribution center. Perhaps you are making websites for people at night. All these require your personal investment of time into the end product. What I want to point out about this type of business is that it's selling yourself. Without you, the business will fall apart or flat out not exist. In effect, it's selling yourself just like you do during your day job – and although it provides additional security, it doesn't give you the freedom to walk away and to have it continue working on its own. It must transform into one of the other types of startups before that happens.

Maybe you found a market niche and are expanding it? Perhaps your evenings are spent building a prototype of the product you are launching or the app you are developing. This kind of business is where you are building on your confidence in a product or service. When you finish standing up the application, or patent the prototype, you don't personally need to do anything else other than maintenance – now you are able to manage the product instead of working for or on the product. Ensuring that your end state has you managing the product, not producing it, is key to becoming a successful part-time startup. While starting up a business that you have to constantly work on is incredible, because it can give you confidence and security, it doesn't give you freedom.

So, let's recap.

1. Building a business or a side hustle gives you confidence and some security – because you are or will always be the primary contributor. If something happens to you, your business might fail.

2. Building an end product or application is intensive in the beginning, yet has an end state that will eventually give you security, confidence, and freedom – the three pillars we are seeking to build with our business. This requires confidence

up front, and can be trying, but can also be the most rewarding.

3. Building a nest for retirement is about minimizing your actual touch time to the key elements required, and also focusing your efforts where they make the most value. This takes the least amount of time, builds the slowest, and is typically going to be best for someone who is investing heavily in their career while still looking for that startup business on the side. This is also going to be more capital intensive, as you will be investing in this business much longer than you would other businesses.

As you think about your startup, consider what you want, and how it will affect your end goal. Do you want minimal investment but are willing to do the work yourself all the time? Are you looking to develop something until you don't need to work on it all the time, and can manage it? Or, are you looking for minimal touch time, but are willing to continue to invest over time into the business?

What It Means to Start a Business with the End in Mind

Long story short – plan your exit strategy from the business up front. Do you have a partner? Spend a long time discussing what happens if the business fails. This is going to be the best time you could have spent when working with a business partner.

A man was starting up a business and working the contracts with their well-funded partner. He spent $70,000 having attorneys draft the contracts with the end in mind so that they could be set up in the best way possible. His well-funded partner? Spent ten times as much! When it all came to a final agreement, the one who spent more won key things in the contract. Not surprisingly, a few years later, despite the company doing well, the partner needed to sell and part ways. Because of the agreements in the contract up front, they knew exactly what was going to happen, and the parting of ways took a little bit of effort, but went extremely smoothly.

Let's consider another partnership with two brothers running a restaurant business. Both were investing different things: one, time as the chef, and the other, a significant chunk of the cash. When the restaurant failed a few years later, it failed with resentment between the brothers – as they hadn't planned what to do if the end came to them. Instead, they argued about who was to blame, what failed, and how things fell apart. This means that they hadn't had clean responsibilities set up at the beginning. As a result, some of the things broke apart in the business because they hadn't clearly defined accountability either.

The value of starting with the end in mind is that it helps assess the risk of the business up front. If you try to review every way you are going to fail, you have the opportunity to overcome those issues before they come to fruition. In effect, you get to ensure that you are planning ahead by reviewing the risks and starting to address them before they even come about! Planning is paramount to the success of your career and your business. Have I mentioned that yet?

PART I – The Part-Time Startup: Building Your Business

Fundamentally, when we talk about starting with the end in mind, we're talking about knowing where the end goal is for all involved. Each day, when you wake up, set the goal of where your desired direction, destination, and end result lands. If you do this at the start of any project, or task, you will always be successful in getting there. When is the last time you went to the grocery store? Did you go with specific items in mind, or did you go to shop? When you go in for just three items, how often do you walk out with four? Or five? Or a full cart and an empty wallet? Even things in our daily lives have a mission, and a vision. Going to the grocery store, I always go with a few items on my mission list, and my vision is to get anything I need that didn't make it on my initial list.

How much are you going to invest of your time, money, or effort? This kind of decision is going to help you understand how much you are going to need to balance. Is the business you are building going to be labor intensive? What are you willing to value your time at while you are working?

For myself, I wanted to build a solid foundation, with minimal effort, but maximum control. As a result, my vision was to spend just a couple of hours a week on normal weeks, have my effort be focused on management and strategy, and the money to be coming from my personal investments, continually infusing my personal money into my business until it hit a point where it could be managed by a part-time staff person instead of an outsourced management team.

Starting with the end in mind applies to more than just a business! When is the last time you were on a diet? Never? Well, really? For the rest of us, we always put ourselves on diets. The question we need to ask is, what is the goal of the diet? Is it to feel better? Maybe you have the goal my spin instructor always pushed: to "look better naked!" Depending on the goal, you may have totally different approaches. Deciding where you will find the finish line will help guide you successfully towards that goal.

Partners in Business – A Good Idea?

Let me start with simple advice: don't get into business with friends and family, unless you are willing to have your relationship with them end. Way too many startups fail and the failure is something that will negatively impact any relationships involved. The less you involve friends and family in a business endeavor, the more likely you are to succeed.

If you have ever watched the movie "8 Mile," Eminem embodies this when he talks about how he thinks he needs to do this on his own. That was the point when he realized that his friends were holding him back, and that if he wanted something he was going to need to step up and do it himself. His friends may have been talking about the vision they had to "get all the bitches" and getting Bentley's and Benjamin's. His moment was realizing that he needed to buy his own time in the studio. That he needed to plan on making himself successful first, and if his music made him more successful, then he would win!

There are five things to have in place to make your partnership work:

❖ **Clear expectations.** As you talk to your new partner, set your expectations. If you run out of money, who is responsible for getting more? How do you decide you need more? Who has the final say in a disagreement? It will also help you avoid disagreements and complications over which partner should handle what. Growth may have meant that each person has done whatever was needed for the company to succeed. For your partnership to succeed, however, you must clearly define responsibilities.

❖ **Partnership agreements.** Not having the right agreements in place can tank your business. It's important to have those agreements written out with an attorney to help ensure success. With clear expectations come clear agreements – spend some time sitting down with your partner and discuss this.

❖ **Mutual benefits.** This might seem obvious, but you both need to be getting something out of it, otherwise it won't be successful. If you both don't get things out of it, you will struggle to work together, and build the business together. If one of you has a much lower benefit then the other, the commitment can come into question, and the business can be dependent on one person verses the other.

❖ **An understanding that it's okay to walk away**. Yes! Amazingly, walking away might be the only way we are able to survive the wrong partnership, and survive when we are building a business. If it isn't right, it isn't right, and it's okay to walk away. Think about a house you are trying to buy. If the price is $300,000 for a $100,000 house, you are okay walking away from it because why would you buy a $100,000 house for three times that much! Other times it can be much more subtle; your business idea may be to run an ethically sourced coffee stand, knowing it will be at the sacrifice of revenue, while they are willing to sacrifice the sourcing in favor of increased income. Subtle disagreements like that can snowball, undermining the company and the growth with conflicting direction.

You both need to be on the same page, for instance, if they are key to the business because of the relationships they have, and they tell you they won't use those relationships, it's time to walk away!

❖ **Continuous thinking about your clients.** Knowing what your strengths are can help balance your business, and knowing how your weaknesses impact your clients can help make our partners more critical. Are you horrible with customer service, and they are amazing? Make sure your roles are clearly defined, so that you can balance your weaknesses as much as possible.

Do you think a partnership is going to be helpful? Truly evaluate every aspect of the partnership you want to create. The integrity of your company will be in the integrity of the partner you choose to work with. How honest are they, and are they transparent in who they are and how they work?

How to Operate a Lean Business

Have you ever been hiking with a group? Ever watched how you always end up having one group go really fast and another really slow? And you always end up spreading out over time as you walk.

Now, put the slowest person in front. The fast folks in the back end up getting annoyed and offering to help the slowest person in front, taking the load off their back, and helping them go faster. By the time it is done, the person in front will have no extra water or backpacks, and everyone will be walking along at the fastest they can as a single group.

In a business, it's important to build a strong culture of lean, which is to say, constant change.

Let's start by building a business based on a few tips:

➢ **Copying is both good and bad.** You are starting a new business, and copying is good, but identical

PART I – The Part-Time Startup:
Building Your Business

copying is bad. If you tried to enter the iphone market, you are competing in an area you won't win – going head to head isn't the right way to take market share. Taking the exact spot that another company is in isn't good. There always has to be something unique or different that sets you apart from something that exists. Where their business model might be perfect for them, small changes might be perfect for you. Hypothetically, if you could take the iphone's design, and made it work on an android, you might find a niche market of people who hate apple, but love the look. This simultaneously might be giving you an incredible market by copying, while having made the adjustment, you made the otherwise non existent market exist.

➢ **Look ahead and anticipate change**. You are starting a business and the market changes all the time. The initial market you thought was perfect may disappear into smoke as soon as you start down that road. Adapt and overcome – avoid falling in love with your business model, because if you want to be successful, it will change over, and over and over and over again!

➢ **Understand the central point of your business**. When building a business, we spoke about the different types of businesses you can build, but we didn't talk about how different types of business models have different central points of income.

❖ There is the resource-driven business. This is where you have an existing asset, and you try to turn it into a business. Own a house and are moving? Rent it out, and this is now a resource driven business! How about that pickup you have, which you can put a plow on the front of during winter?

❖ There is the offer-driven business. This is where you are working within a current process, and you have a value-added proposition to improve the customer's major points of frustration or cost. Think about a grocery delivery service; one group of customers wasn't worried about price but didn't like driving out to the store all the time. This business found the in between and addressed the process of purchasing groceries and eliminated the need to drive there.

- ❖ A customer-driven business is an extremely common one. Want to start making soap and selling it? The customer is who the business is all about and making them happy is critical for your success. Every restaurant you've ever been to, every store you've bought from, are all living in this central business model.

- ❖ Finally, there is the financial-driven business, where you are innovating something in the industry, as to how the industry is charging, or operating. A solar panel set placed on a home has multiple options for financing, and each one was an innovation in the finance industry. Perhaps you have been building a cash business, and you added the option to accept a credit card? Or perhaps you started selling online? That additional revenue is a new business that wouldn't have existed for you otherwise.

➢ **Iterate often**. Know that your business will constantly evolve, and if you iterate often you will find that you will constantly adapt and evolve when others are not. It helps you keep your income stream and makes sure that you don't accidently go down the wrong path. Two things should be constantly in your mind: being agile and being lean. When you are trying to understand a revenue stream, map out each step that it takes to make money. This value stream map will help you understand the core of your business.

➢ Build your customer into your product. Conduct research, but include more than just what they say from the feedback you get. Even as a small startup, you can conduct market research without spending a lot of money. Understanding your customer is helpful when you understand them at their core, which is where you can stand out. What do they like to do during weekends? What influences them? What do you know about their attitude in public? What does success mean to them? What worries them? These are questions to help you understand how a customer is at their core. The better you understand your customer, the better you can adapt and overcome your competition. Large companies are constantly trying to understand their customers, and they attempt to use as much data as possible, but if you can understand your customers not just as statistics, but rather at the core of who they are, you may find you have an edge over your competition.

Making Success Mundane

This is going to sound really counter intuitive. Many folks will recommend celebrating often, even the little successes. When you're managing a team of people this can be incredibly helpful. Let's talk about how to avoid losing momentum because of success.

First, you won't have something big and new come up every day. It's great to be able to talk to people about success all the time, and be able to say, "We're about to announce a big partnership." Those days are great, just like the days when you are able to say, "We just raised several million dollars in funding." My favorite is when you lock up a major customer. But as much as we'd love to say that this happens every day, it doesn't, and it won't.

PART I – The Part-Time Startup:
Building Your Business

But this is a marathon. Do you know the difference between the winners of marathons and those who are close? The winners push themselves to the maximum of their body's capability the entire time, with upwards of 95% of prolonged exertion. Those that come close, push their bodies hard but only get to about 90%. The difference is in how they trained. The winner trained in sprints, becoming incredibly good at those short sprints, making them longer each time, eventually able to sprint the entire marathon. Those that came close? They started by jogging the distance, then running it the entire time.

Starting a business isn't something you get into for kicks – it is something you get into with a prolonged passion, and the desire to sprint the entire way.

Imagine yourself as a drug dealer. You might be able to make a lot of money in a big sale, but ultimately, you are sprinting, then stopping, then sprinting again – all while doing something illegal. Well, apparently in California it's not illegal to sell pot!

Now, let's take that job at Panda Express making minimum wage. You get a steady paycheck, and aren't going to make a ton of money, but you might eventually. Well, believe it or not, your job at Panda Express is a marathon; *and* you are making more than most drug dealers on top of it when you break it down by the hour.

When you look at your startup, everything you have done to build yourself is making your sprints longer than before, slowly building up, until you are able to sprint the entire marathon. The ability to sprint the entire time, while everyone else is running, makes the difference between a winner, and a runner up.

Having the ability to make success mundane is the way you will get your startup ahead. It isn't about being amazing once – it's about being able to do the same thing over and over and over again that will make you successful. Ever heard of the movie star The Rock (aka Dwayne Johnson)? Do you know how much he works out every day to look the way he does? And how disciplined his diet is? He isn't just "that buff." Instead, he works every day to look that strong, and be that strong. All that work may make his success seem mundane to him, because it is just what he does and who he is.

The more you can make your daily routine compliment your goals, the more you will be able to succeed. And you will be doing it as part of your natural self-expression. Building your skills and tools to compliment your mission and vision will help you wake up every day already able to be successful. In turn, making your success boring, which is when you know you've made it.

Choosing Mentors – the Revolving Wheel of Trust and Guidance

Have you ever asked yourself how to find a mentor? Or perhaps you've felt nervous about reaching out to a mentor because they are "too big." Let's start with the rules you need to start with when approaching a mentor:

- ➢ Be efficient with their time - don't waste their time, come with an agenda and execute it.
- ➢ Come prepared with questions – make the meeting focused on what you want to learn and get out of them.
- ➢ Don't expect that you will be able to meet with them regularly.
- ➢ Confidentiality is a must.
- ➢ Make sure that there is a no-fault end of the relationship.
- ➢ Ask them how you can help them.

Mentors come and go in your career, and you should be okay with that. Learn about them, their background, and then find ways to make it specifically valuable for you, and for them. Each mentor is a door filled with information, and there

PART I – The Part-Time Startup:
Building Your Business

are many out there. Choose one, learn all you can, then open another, then another, then another. Do you remember the text books you occasionally picked up to remind yourself of how to do things? Each of these relationships can help with that, and each of these doors has more doors inside to help you learn more.

So set up a rhythm and figure out how often you need to talk to a mentor, or how often you want to find a new mentor. Monthly? Weekly? Did you set it up where you will only be going to them for support when you are stumped with a problem? Build your network of mentors and utilize them when you need them.

Part II – LIFE:
Balancing Your Personal
Commitments

Life Happens – How Bad Do You Want It?

This is a pretty short section, in part on purpose. It is also short because simply put, what you are doing is going to make this balance tough.

One of the challenges with balancing your life is that, honestly, life happens. While we have already gone over how 'choice' impacts so much of your success, sometimes you don't feel like you have a choice.

The reality is that no matter what, you always have that choice, whether you believe it or not. Sometimes unexpected things do happen that significantly impact you, such as a spouse dying, parents who are ill, siblings who need help, or the needs of your kids.

As these situations come up, own them. During one interview for this book, a woman mentioned how she had an unplanned pregnancy and a child, using that as justification for what happened to throw the initial trajectory of her life off. During conversation, we discussed her choices prior and her choices after she was pregnant. At each stage, she recognized that she was responsible for the decisions she made, and that she could have made dramatically different decisions.

Then another woman talked about how she had a truly unplanned child – the woman had taken every precaution possible, then had made the decision to keep the child. Further in the discussion, we talked about whether adoption had been a consideration, and while she assured me adamantly that she would not go back and change her mind, she reflected on why she hadn't seriously considered it. As a single mother she had so much change in her life, and it made the balance in life extremely difficult.

Part II – LIFE:
Balancing Your Personal Commitments

Both of these illustrate how much choice is still part of the equation, even when you don't think it is. In life, you have to consider what is important to you. That is why we started off understanding your mission and vision. These will guide your priorities, but also help determine your ability to adapt to unplanned changes as they come.

One person spoke about how cancer impacted their life. They spoke about how their first wife, then brother, nephews, and most recently, son, have died in the past few years in rapid succession as well. As they spoke about it, tears were welling up in their eyes, and they talked about how these things impacted them.

This man was profoundly impacted by each of these changes, and as we spoke, we talked about his mission in life, and whether it had changed. What we discovered during our discussion, was that he had not changed when his wife died. His mission hadn't changed. His vision hadn't changed. The same was the case when his son died.

Then we talked about how cancer had changed him. We went from being sad about his family no longer being with us, to impacted because he was no longer able to be the same person that he had been. He was physically limited because of the cancer he had fought and won and although he was proud to be free of it, he talked about how he was never actually going to be free of it. His limitations deeply impacted him, and changed his outlook on life and his mission and vision had changed. How we respond to these deeply impactful situations will change how we respond to the world. So how bad do we want it?

For those reading this, let's pause and watch a video where we listen to Eric Thomas talk. You can watch the video here: https://www.youtube.com/watch?v=lsSC2vx7zFQ&t=9s.

For those listening, I'll give you a summary. The story is about a guru teaching a guy how to be successful. When the guy shows up, on a beach in a suit, the guru says to wade out into the water. When the guy is waist deep, the guru says to keep going. Going out until his head is under water. You have to want to succeed more than you want to breathe if you want to get ahead. When your desire to succeed is the same as your desire to breathe, you will have the drive and energy to make sure you can get ahead of anything that life throws your way.

Part II – LIFE:
Balancing Your Personal Commitments

As we look at the horrific, painful and terrifying things that life can throw at us, ask, do they change our mission? How badly do we want to be successful? Do we feel the need to change it and resist? Do you want your mission more than you want to breathe?

Work-Life Balance Is a Myth

Yes, work-life balance is a myth. That's because it's not a balance; it's an integration of work and life, especially in today's world. Maybe in the 1920s you might have been able to have a work life and a home life, but these days, very few careers allow a clear separation between these two.

And who would want that anyway? Wouldn't you rather work with your friends and family? Or work with people who become part of your family, at least? The more you integrate your work life and home life, the more impactful it is to how you feel in your life. Want to have a late meeting? Invite the person over for dinner! Not only can you potentially reduce conflicts, but you can humanize yourself and

Part II – LIFE:
Balancing Your Personal Commitments

enjoy your meeting more with the person. Your family gets to experience you, both as you are at home and as you are at work, and your children get to be exposed to the whole you.

Or would you rather I talked about time-management techniques so that you aren't working 80 hours a week? Later we'll look at a few of those, but for now, let's talk about how work is not the opposite of life. Instead, it is part of life, similar to how family is part of life, friends are part of life, and your community, your hobbies, and your home are part of life.

Two nurse practitioners doing the exact same job talked about what made them enjoy their job the most. One talked about being able to connect with patients, talking to them about their families, their lives. It brought them joy in knowing that they were bringing people back to those lives. The other found love in making sure that the patient had exactly what they needed, in prescribing things, and in discovering what was wrong with a person.

These two were driven by different activities in their lives. We want those driving factors to be able to help us focus. We want to go to work every day and be invigorated by that work. We want to be able to weave these things we love into our lives. By doing so, we will find that 80 hour weeks are more bearable, and we are able to find energy and love in our life while we perform those long weeks.

Here is your homework: for the next week, carry a notepad with you, and choose two pages, one marked "loved it," and the other "loathed it." When you go to a meeting that you run, and you love it, put that meeting down on the "loved it" page. Did you love going to the gym? Put it down. Write down everything you experience in a week. Perhaps put a star next to the things you do at work and that end up on the "loved it" page, so that you can see how your work and home are currently balanced.

At the end of this week, spend some time reflecting on the loved and loathed. Now see what we can do to remove or reduce the parts that we loathe. Do you loathe the hour-long drive to work? Or do you love it because it's the only quiet time you get all day? As you look at your list, this is how you can make small changes to what you do on a daily basis in order to improve your ability to integrate your work and home life. Oh, and as a side note, this is a technique used by doctors and has shown about a 20% reduction in "burnout."

Part II – LIFE:
Balancing Your Personal Commitments

This works because a vast majority of us (almost 80%) have the ability to change some aspects of what we do for work. Yet only about 15% actually take advantage of this ability, and do it! What is wrong with us?! We just keep working, and doing things we loathe, when we have power and control over making changes in our career to make ourselves happier! If you don't enjoy doing something at work, talk to your boss about it, and see if you can remove or reduce it! You might find, to your surprise, that they can make what you hate about your job go away!

How Do You Balance It All?

There are a lot of tools and things we can do to help balance work, life, and the startup you're trying to create.

Let's start with the first one: stop being a perfectionist. Do you know how many times I just wrote crap before editing this book, throwing it away, rewriting it, and praying that my editor would make it not totally suck? A perfectionist can never finish what they are doing, because there is always opportunity to change, or improve what they did. What you should consider is what do you need to do to get to 90% of what perfection would look like to you. That B+ in college got you a degree and balanced learning. Heck, if you got a 4.0 or a 5.0 GPA, what didn't you learn, or didn't you do because you spent all of your time studying? Letting go of perfectionist tendencies will be powerful and allow you to balance your time more effectively.

Part II – LIFE:
Balancing Your Personal Commitments

Unplug! When was the last time you put your phone down for an hour (aside from when you were asleep)? Unplugging can be powerful in helping reduce distractions. It can allow you to focus more effectively than multitasking allows. Speaking of multitasking, how often do you multitask? Never? Really? If you are listening to this on audible, you are definitely not being truthful, because you are totally driving, walking, or making dinner. I know I am when I'm listening!

Have you ever been told you are multitasking to failure? Let's say you have one project on your plate to execute. How well and quickly are you going to execute that project? How about when you have 20 projects? Are you cutting corners and being less effective? That is called multitasking to failure.

Instead of managing those 20 projects, perhaps you can:

Studies show that multitasking ends up reducing your overall productivity, and when we are talking about trying to find the most efficient way of managing our time, and integrating our life and work together, does it make sense to be less efficient? Of course not!

This isn't to say that you can't balance multiple projects at once, but making sure that you spend the time to focus on those projects and finish them before grabbing your next one will greatly improve your ability to accomplish goals that you set in a timely manner.

Part II – LIFE:
Balancing Your Personal Commitments

Meditation and exercise, as mentioned in the previous section, can greatly impact and assist in your ability to be effective and to effectively manage your time. Have you noticed how Google and others have built pods for their employees to have 'quiet time?' They found, like you will, that sometimes taking a break away from your work, will give you strategy, clearer thinking, and make you see things you won't otherwise see in building your business.

Limiting time-wasting activities can be a huge benefit when you focus things. If you have a 30-minute meeting, make sure it's packed full of agenda topics so you are never bored. Furthermore, if you can end it in 15 minutes, do it! If you have a meeting that you find painful and doesn't add value, ask yourself how can you make it better? Remember, as you do this sometimes those long and painful meetings have a really good reason for being that way, so you need to consider all areas and ask yourself how it can be more effective.

Also, limit your exposure to time-wasting people. During an interview for this book, a man started talking and kept on digressing away from the questions being asked. Because the goal was to listen and learn any nuggets of information that might influence this book, the conversation kept going nowhere. After three hours with this person, I made a slight edit to the phrasing of one sentence. That's a horribly small change considering the commitment I made. I still can't believe how I allowed my time to be consumed like that.

This means you must also master patience, because patience in those situations is invaluable to presenting yourself, learning, and growing. Focus on learning to balance between being a listening, and

Part II – LIFE:
Balancing Your Personal Commitments
cutting to the chase so you can get the most value in the least amount of time.

The last thing you can do to balance it all, is to change your habits. You will learn which habits limit you, as well as learn to accept that change is always possible and present. However, we aren't talking about big changes to your habits. You won't be successful jumping in and making *huge* changes. If you said you were deciding to bike ride 30 miles a night, you are going to fail. On the other hand, you can start with one mile a night. Then push it to two. Remember, IBM didn't come out with the Pentium 4, without the Pentium 3 first. and the new iPhone didn't jump into being an iPhone 10, without going through one thru nine. When you are done, the habit you are developing stays with you, and those small changes changed your life, your work, and the integration and balance of both.

Balancing as a Parent

Let me just start with a huge caveat – you might find a lot more value reading books from people who have kids. I have four cats and two dogs, which means I am woefully underqualified to write this, but did find insights from folks interviewed. So, let's see just how much you hate the insight by the end of this chapter. You've been warned!

The first thing I've been told is that balancing as a parent can get extremely difficult if you have a career and a business to manage. This is truly where integrating your life can be of high value. Let's say you're part-time business has to do with child care – now you have a logical and easy integration of family time and business, especially if your kids are of the same age as your child care clients. But let's say your business isn't like that.

To balance this business as a single parent, you are going to need to really look at how time intensive your business is. Even a child care business is going to constantly be taking time from your own children, because you will have to spend time with other children. So the first thing you should do is be open about the situation with everyone. When your family

Part II – LIFE:
Balancing Your Personal Commitments

is aware of the scope of your career and ambitions, they can make accommodations to greatly help you integrate everything. A single person can't lift a heavy table, but ten people can lift a small bit of it, and it becomes easier.

Setting expectations with those you work with will dramatically help as well. If you need to pick up your children at 5 p.m. every day and have to leave at 4:30 p.m. to get there, then set that as the expectation. This doesn't mean that you aren't willing to put in the hours. It means that if your job occasionally needs late nights, than you need to have a discussion about how you will make those hours or time-sensitive deadlines up since late nights aren't an option. Could you get in at 4 a.m. on the days that need the extra time instead of getting in at 8 a.m.? Maybe you won't be able to support those super-fast, two-day turnaround jobs, but you can support things that go into the weekend, as you'll put hours in on Saturday and Sunday. These expectations will evolve as your child evolves, so it's best to keep everyone in your life included in how things change.

Make sure you are focused, and produce good, quality work when you are in the office. Even the most understanding companies still want you to actually produce, and as a result, be at work when you are at work, unless an emergency happens. If you need to put in extra hours due to dropping off and picking up your kid, see if you can get a laptop and put in a few hours of work during the evening from home.

Merge your work and home calendars. This is good practice for everyone! A single calendar can make a huge difference in your success, as your time management will be all in one place. When your calendar becomes extremely busy, you even have to put travel time in between meetings, to the airport, any commute time you have, and more. Integrating your life together is realizing that you aren't living two lives; you are living just the one!

Delegate and accept help! When family and friends offer to help, say yes! You aren't showing weakness if you do this. Rather, you are showing the strength to know your own time limitations and to recognize the commitments that you can and cannot make.

At work, delegating as a supervisor not only helps you grow your team better, but will also create a more effective team. An intern can do an expense report. Your employee can write a draft of the letter that needs to go out. Eventually, they will be able to follow these actions through without your assistance, giving you more time to balance your commitments. Delegation is going to be your friend at every step of your life.   You will be able to accomplish more, empower teams better, delivering the same amount *or more*, with less time spent on it!

PART III -

WORK: Building Yourself

and Your Career

Starting off Right – How Your Decisions Early on Can Make All the Difference

Now, onto the first lesson that isn't about building a business. Let's start back in middle school. Do you remember your time there? Well, I do, and I hated it. Remember those miserable, teenage years when you found yourself wondering if life would get better?

Of course, you are reading this book now, and you're probably not in middle school. So, you already know the truth – life doesn't get better. It gets worse. Much worse. Now don't get me wrong, you will have some high points in your life. Your first kiss. Your first time driving a car. Maybe that time when you got a hickey and your mother saw it and just laughed before offering you concealer. The first time you got made fun of for wearing concealer, and you realized you should have just 'owned' it. Well, we all know how our early years can help frame things for your future. So, here is the first question for you to ponder: have you started yourself out right?

I know, most of this is not going to be within your control, so don't fret about it. I started with a middle school analogy because maybe you are a parent, an aunt, an uncle, or just someone in the peanut gallery and you'll see that this lesson can be learned retroactively, as well as applied early to those within your influence.

The bottom line is that the early decisions must revolve around providing you with challenges you will rise to. Some people say things like, "Will you rise to the challenge?" But the part missing from that cliché is asking if that challenge is really something you want to rise to? If it was, did you? Or did you sit passively and watch the world go by as a spectator?

PART III -

WORK: Building Yourself and Your Career

For myself, I hated school. But I loved math, and because of that love I was put into the gifted class. Did I like repeating the same problem over and over? No, of course not, but I loved being able to finish a problem and have that mini victory before going on to the next one. This allowed me to rise to the challenge, and these small victories gave me courage, passion, and drive.

When someone gave me a book, I either loved it or hated it. I devoured the things that I loved. Take the Harry Potter books as an example. I consumed them so quickly I wouldn't stop until the book was finished. Six hundred pages? Six hundred minutes of reading? Ha! That was nothing. I didn't need caffeine, I read in the dark, and just kept at it – I rose to the challenge, and devoured it like a conquering hero.

So, when you look at yourself, whether you *are* in middle school, high school, in college, or are moving into middle age, ask yourself: what challenge do you rise to? These are the passions you have and can nurture.

Rising to the challenge starts with the decisions you make. One recurring theme you'll hear in this book is that choice and decisions are critical for success.

High school, for many of us, is the first chance for us to see our own choices standing out. Did we choose to join a sports team? Math club? Theater? To use today's terminology, did we choose to be a "try hard"? If we didn't, that's okay, too. Not everyone was the misfit jock / choir boy / Eagle Scout / nerd / geek / outcast / audiovisual guy I was. I want you to reflect on the concept of challenging yourself when you were in high school. What did you do that was hard?

This is a moment for you to pause and reflect on things that get you excited.

While you reflect, here are some personal examples: I played video games. A lot. Like, a lot a lot. Maybe too much. No, it was definitely too much. I became addicted, not with games themselves, but addicted to the challenge that competing with people gave me. The community and friends I made online had me hooked. Did video games get in the way of my studies and other stuff? Maybe. But I approached those other things with passion as well. When you reflect on your choices, did you choose to have passion in something? What doors did you choose to walk through, why, and how?

PART III -
WORK: Building Yourself and Your Career

Outside of class I pushed myself, too. I didn't go home and watch TV (okay, I did, but I did it after these things). I joined the track team, and the wrestling team, and the football team, and found small bits of passion and challenges in these as well. Ok, I did my homework while watching South Park, just, don't tell my mom.

But why are decisions so important? Looking back, I joined football because my parents encouraged me, and because I wanted to be that big football player out there – I wanted to be strong and awesome. But freshman year, I didn't do wrestling, and I almost didn't do track. It was after a season without them that I make the choice, the decision. To keep challenging myself by being involved above and beyond 'just' school. I pushed myself in Scouting, pushed myself by being involved in activities, and kept pushing myself to stay out of my comfort zone, so that I could keep learning more, faster and better than those around me who weren't engaged. My goal wasn't to get 100% on my math tests – instead, my goal was to get an 90% on *every* test, including the tests that school didn't offer – like learning teamwork, leadership, community involvement and other things. By being able to experience so much, I make myself proficient at many things, even if it meant I would never get 100% on all of my math tests.

So, when we talk about starting early, I want you to reflect on your early decisions. What made you decide to do the things you do? What challenges did you take? What did you do to push yourself above and beyond? Remember, we are looking at building a business, and if you aren't passionate about it, you won't do it. If you can't find what you are passionate about, you will find yourself floundering like a fish.

And I love Sushi, but I don't want it to smell fishy, if you know what I mean.

Education Matters - As Does Your Choice in Degrees and Extracurricular Activities

When we talk about education we have to be honest. Your choices can make or break your opportunities in the future. Although we're told that we can always restart, go back to school, and change what we are "educated" in, more often than not what we actually find is that we end up in situations where we can't go back.

"Life happens" as the saying goes. When you are working, you may not be able to take time off to go back to school for two, three, or four years. Moreover, you may not be in a situation where you feel comfortable getting a student loan. Or, as often happens, going back to school for a bachelor's degree might be perceived negatively or as a frivolous waste, depending on your social circle. Facing that backlash and lack of encouragement, it can be easier to just not go back at all.

So, how do we make sure you are making the right choice in school? Honestly, it all depends on what you want to do, and the passions you have. Let's talk about some examples that happen frequently. Patent attorneys need a degree in engineering, and that first choice to be an engineer before an attorney makes the difference in their ability to be in that career.

How about working in engineering? Well, the degree you choose can make a huge impact in how you are judged and considered for your next job. A degree in mechanical engineering might get you overlooked for electrical engineering roles. A degree in electrical engineering may get you overlooked for a

PART III -
WORK: Building Yourself and Your Career

mechanical engineering role. Every choice you have in college can make a difference.

Let's look at business administration, which is a common degree in schools today. What does this degree train you to do? Is it making you a generalist? Are you too general? And more importantly, did you look at the job market for folks with BA degrees? Your bachelor's degree is the base framework from which you will view all things later.

Communications is a degree that many people look into, because communication is so important in everything we do. Can you imagine reading this book if you couldn't communicate?

I understand that people choose communication because people are looking to be in advertising, news reporting, or other things. Now, let's consider that degree against a degree in English. Are you limiting yourself by choosing communications if you later decide that you are passionate about teaching? What kind of careers do you want to make sure you keep the doors open for when you're looking for your first job?

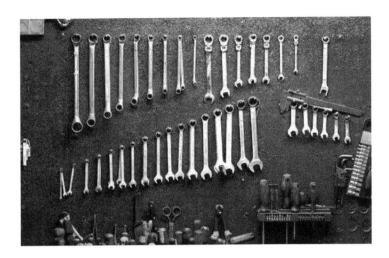

One way to think about this is to ask yourself, what are the set of tools that you want to make sure you are prepared with? Let's say you're asked to build a house. Do you want to be prepared with the ability to shingle the house in addition to framing it, for instance? What about electrical installation and plumbing? Are you going to have the skills to do that work, too? Everything you do with your education is a choice you are making around the tools that you will carry with you in the future. And occasionally, it isn't about the tools you will learn, it is the tools that people *perceive* you have learned.

PART III -
WORK: Building Yourself and Your Career

That said, education isn't always formal! You may be incredible at something because you grew up around it or had a mentor train you. That training may be far better than you could have gotten formally, but now you need to consider the perspective of those who are going to be looking at your education. Are they going to take it seriously that you know something because you have been doing it since you were 10? More likely that will ask what you have done "professionally."

This is where. education, and your choices in education, really matter. An experienced engineer once told me they hadn't graduated high school, and they didn't need to, because why would they need to, they had 30 years of experience! A few months later, they found out that they couldn't climb any higher in the corporate ladder without their degree. They chose, and in their case, they had no financial barriers in their way.

In addition to adding to your toolkit, you are also balancing perceptions of those around you. So, let's digress a little bit and talk about education that isn't a degree. You may be sitting here thinking about how you have been trained in tons of stuff that didn't result in a degree or a certification. So, what does that mean for you? It means you need to find a way to either prove you know what you are doing, or, more likely, you need to find a way that proves your knowledge.

For example, if you grew up fixing cars with your uncle, and as a result you know an astronomical amount about cars, well, how do you portray that knowledge to others as an employable or marketable skill? Do you say it like I just said it? Do you share it as a hobby? How do you let someone know you have that vast resource of knowledge?

It's all about understanding who your intended audience is. Is it a friend who you tell everything? Or is it a potential employer or teammate? This isn't about lying, but knowing when the truth can be

PART III -
WORK: Building Yourself and Your Career

presented in a better way. Reviewing it from the perspective of the other person, and presenting it with that in mind.

Your uncle may have been fixing up cars just for himself. You might tell your close friends about how it was a hodge-podge setup. However, how many cars did you work on? Did you only fix one thing, or many things? Changed tires? Replaced exhaust components? Changed out seating? Painted? Welded? Replaced sparkplugs? When you present this in a private manner you might present it as just doing what your uncle said, and how he said it. However, when you present it in a professional light, you were working in an auto repair shop. Do they need to know that it was a family business? Is that going to strengthen the communication of the value of that education? It's all in how you frame your experience. Now consider this as it applies to your startup – how you frame yourself and manage the perceptions of others can make or break your success.

Perhaps you had an internship? When you are working with professionals, do they take the word internship in a positive light? Or perhaps you look at it as opportunities for professional development: a practical place where you got to focus your education. Sharing how you developed your professional experience, verses 'having an internship' can be perceived very differently. So, what is your choice? This is about knowing who you are, as much as knowing who you want to be, and how your education helps shape you. Remember, the choices made here help to shape your initial toolkit, but they also help to shape how others view you.

Your choices about extracurricular activities make a difference as well. Let's say you chose to join an organization that you were passionate about, but that was polarizing in some company. So, how do you make this work? Does it work? Will it help you or hurt you? Your associations need to go above you, beyond you, and have you reflecting on who and what you want to be perceived as, as well as develop into.

PART III -
WORK: Building Yourself and Your Career

Some examples: when going to school, did you join a professional society? Was it an honors society? A service organization? Or a fraternity/sorority? Did you think that those in the latter might create a polarizing network? Some people don't get in where they wanted to get in. Others find that they lost friends or were shunned due to that close fraternity or sorority. So, how did that choice impact you?

What are you doing above and beyond your base schooling to help you understand more about the world? Are you auditing classes you think might be interesting? Are you doing things that will help arm you for the next steps? Me personally, I audited business classes while getting my degree in engineering. I've gotta say, it's pretty interesting when you see all of the folks who dropped out of engineering sitting in the business classes you are auditing. I'm gonna be a snob here and say, they could keep'em.

But what if you are already out of school? Did you know that there are many universities that share their coursework for free online? You might think nothing is free, but I assure you there is a LOT of free educational material online!

https://oyc.yale.edu/ holds, "Open Yale Courses (OYC) provides lectures and other materials from selected Yale College courses to the public free of charge via the Internet."

https://www.edx.org/school/harvardx allows you to, "Browse free online courses in a variety of subjects. Harvard University courses found below can be audited free or students can choose to receive a verified certificate for a small fee."

I'd give you more, but so many universities have and continue to do this and they do it because not many people take advantage of it, but they want to give back to you! You the reader of this book, are the target audience for those universities, so you as the

PART III -

WORK: Building Yourself and Your Career

reader now, can go and take charge of your own learning – even without spending money!

Have you been taking these classes? What about professional affiliations? Are you attending conferences? Learning more? These continuing education tools will fundamentally help you as you navigate balancing, developing, and growing professionally, as well as help you grow your business. They will also help you network to find more mentors, connections, and ways to grow your business.

Searching for Your First Job – the Most Difficult Fight You Have Ever Known

If you are already working, you might have gotten lucky. A family connection, a single application, or something quick might have resulted in you getting a job without a "fight."

Now, let me tell you what you *should* have been doing, if you didn't experience it then.

PART III -
WORK: Building Yourself and Your Career

Apply, apply, apply, apply, apply! But when? Did you start a few months before graduating? Wow, you were late. Whenever you are looking to graduate, you should be applying a year before. Graduating in January? You should have started the previous December. And the key with this is keeping your application tempo the entire year.

Why so many applications and such a hard push to get them out there? Well, this is about giving yourself the best start you can and having options will help you with this. Remember, successful startups start from successful people. Are you limiting your applications to specific locations? Stop that! Everything about this start is setting you up for success.

Remember how we talked about choice? When you went to school, you chose where you went – now you need to consider what else went into that decision. Did you stay local for your family? Was that the right decision then? Is it still? Each choice you made up until now will determine a lot about your first job, and now you need to make sure that you give yourself the best opportunity possible, because we know that it isn't always possible to have gotten here while making every perfect choice.

So, with all of the mistakes you have made, take an honest look at whether you are driving your future. Are you taking control of the things you need to do? If not, how can you start?

The hardest part about looking for your first job is accepting that you can't stop until you are satisfied. That being said, you also have to weigh each choice you make around the jobs you apply for, interviews you accept, and ultimately the position you take or don't take. Sometimes the right move is less transparent than we think. Have your dream job and an offer in hand? Great, but don't get complacent. Take the job, but keep interviewing and applying for others until you are a few months into that dream job. This is about risk management. That dream job may have sounded or seemed perfect when you took

PART III -
WORK: Building Yourself and Your Career

it, but you need to manage your personal risk, keep looking, and maintain a backup plan in case things go south.

Managing risk is an important lesson. You might say that part of succeeding is protecting oneself. Part of the reason you are going to start a business part-time is to manage your risk. For every job change, and every time you are looking for one, the more carefully you manage your risk, the better your life will be.

Let's toss around an example, focusing on a down employment market at graduation. A student graduated with an engineering degree and took an easy job. It didn't pay well (it didn't actually pay at all for the first year), and it wasn't great, but, hey, it was available, and they took the position for "experience." Here's the caveat: this student had a 3.91 GPA from a great university. Now their decision to undersell themselves seems kind of silly. Fast forward ten years: factoring in raises and such, that employee has only been getting paid what they are *actually* worth for about five of their 10 working years. They are way underemployed and way underpaid. However, they *did* make their family happy, while managing to bank quite a bit of money by living at home that entire time.

This person was one of the 14% in their graduating class who graduated with a job, albeit one that didn't pay well, that was only found because of a family connection, and ultimately stunted his or her growth professionally as a result. They stayed underpaid for several years until they moved to a job that paid as much as a college hire was making, a solid five years behind the curve.

Another student graduated with a 2.66 GPA. They hunted for an entire 18 months prior to graduation. They took every effort to hone themselves as an engineer, worked hard, had part-time jobs, and were the most frequent visitor during university at career counselling and resume review services. They applied to more than 600 positions and got dozens of interviews. From those, they prepared, practiced, and managed to get offers from two employers. This person, with a 2.66 GPA, walked out as part of the 7% of graduates who were getting jobs without family connections. They were also among the 3% who had multiple offers at graduation. A 2.66 GPA student was able to start out much stronger than a 3.91GPA student. Pretty amazing.

These two examples highlight the key difference: drive and preparedness can make the difference between someone who wouldn't have gotten a job otherwise and someone who walked out with multiple offers in an incredibly tough market.

The example above demonstrated a challenging environment when the market was difficult. After all, 14% of graduating engineers that year had jobs from that specific tier 1 university, an extreme low. Now let's talk about that same preparedness in an up market.

Before I give an example, though, do you see how this kind of planning could be equally beneficial in that up market?

At a different university, engineers were leaving the university with a guarantee of employment. The market was extremely competitive. As a result, most engineers had offers well before graduating, because the companies came onto campus, solicited them, and placed them quickly and effectively.

So, in one example, a person got hired the exact same way – they had a family connection, and they were able to get an offer at a large aerospace company with one interview. Boom: job search done. They got a great starting salary and a pretty good position, though in a less than ideal location. That's okay, though, and the employee didn't care, because they had connections which they thought they would use to help rise to a CEO level in five years. Ha, yea right.

PART III -

WORK: Building Yourself and Your Career

The other person went to every job fair on campus, went to several professional conferences, and did the same extensive planning as the prior example in the down market. They ended up having more than a dozen offers, many overlapping. This person would then accept the best offer, then reassess any time a new offer came in, sometimes weighing multiple offers at once. They didn't stop until they started the job. Even after, they had put so much work in that they ended up having two additional offers while they were working.

This second person took the job hunt with the same rigor and passion in an up market as a down market. Because of that, they started their job making more, enjoyed the job more, got to work in a city they preferred, and ultimately ended up with more potential opportunities.

There's more to this example that's helpful for us to understand. Every time this person interviewed, they interviewed like they needed that job. They were sincere, but they didn't do things like snub an interview when they were told the salary range. They were candid with the person and discussed the positives in the role as they understood them, so they could see each opportunity from the best light. Financially, one offer was much lower than the others they had already received. Instead of saying, "This is much lower, I'm not interested," the person asked about what other benefits there were. It was a smaller company, so they talked about the value of learning more because you have multiple jobs and responsibilities, while in other jobs you might feel like "just a number." They also took the time to learn about the company, including what exactly it did, and asked a lot of questions. Each interview became as much a conversation as it did an interview, making the interviewers enjoy and like the applicant that much more.

This person also didn't take reneging lightly, and every time they had an offer then needed to decline

PART III -
WORK: Building Yourself and Your Career

after accepting another, they wrote an apology e-mail. They didn't highlight the fact that they had gotten a better job, but instead talked about how they appreciated the opportunity but thought they might have found a slightly better fit for themselves elsewhere. Furthermore, they went above and beyond by sending a physical letter to each person they interviewed with as well.

So why am I going into such depth about this example? Simply because that person was able to keep in good standing with all those folks even though they rejected their offers. Then one of the competitors to the company she ultimately decided on sent an unsolicited email to interview for a position. The offer was well above anything she had ever seen, and as a result she walked away making twice her initial salary, which was already much more than the person who used connections had. The persistence, hard work, and honesty gave her options that were not available otherwise.

As you build your start-up, think about what kind of choices you make, and how your brand and energy is used. The brand you are making in your career can make a huge impact and exponentially change the path of your career for better or for worse, just as the brand you make for your company will as well. These two examples show how the planning, preparation, and extra "personal touch" can make your first job search go that much better. As much as we learn in life about math, business, English, physics, French, and music, everything comes back to choice, and people.

PART III -
WORK: Building Yourself and Your Career

I still keep a thank you note from a mentee who shadowed me for a day. It was hand written, left on my desk, and years later, I remember her name. Will your interviewers remember your name? And more importantly, will they remember you years later, and give you a call when they need someone like you? How is your business' brand being perceived?

Choosing the Right Job for You

Choosing the right job when you don't know what you want to do is critical for your next steps. So before we go on, do you know what you want to do? Or do you at least have a rough idea? If your answer is "make money," you at least understand the fundamental goal of every company ever – and a great goal for you to have as well.

PART III -
WORK: Building Yourself and Your Career

But how do you decide when you have no idea what you want to do? When faced with this, we need to get to a root question: what is your *mission*? And then, what is your *vision*? Everything in this book is fundamentally tied to choice, but those choices must guide you towards accomplishing your mission and vision.

My personal mission is to strive to be the best, to make a difference, and to control the aspects of my life that I want to control.

Let's break this mission down into what it looks like in action. I am constantly taking more classes, reading new things, and trying to keep my brain from "getting set in its ways." I use the guidance I was given a long time ago: "give rise to mind while abiding nowhere." To be the best at whatever I set my mind to also means that I need to try to keep different perspectives and challenge them at all times. Am I too American in my thinking? Am I too privileged? What perspective do I need to reflect on to ensure that I continue to strive to be my best self?

Side note: And which came first, the chicken or the egg? Serious question. Did the successful person come first? Or did the successful business idea come first?

Back to my personal mission - as for making a difference, what company do I work for? Do I live by a code that others respect and envy? Do I embody a role model and someone willing to take a stand? I once worked for a company that made unethical decisions, so I left to find something that lived by a better code. Yet it was also important to me to give back with what I was working on. I wanted to make a difference, and it needed to be something meaningful to who I am.

The importance of control in my life is something I learned early on. What I learned was that when I control my life, the only thing I have to fear is my own failure. This means that I am most afraid of myself, but that fear is also something that drives my own success. It impassions me to not let myself down, and it makes sure that I push the edge, develop, and take control. This is also part of the reason why I suspect that many of you are reading this book! Controlling your life, making sure you don't feel like you must always be submissive to your boss, and giving you a sense of control in your life are important goals. If you are successful in your endeavors, and in your balance between your work and your business, you will be able to sit, have a bad week, and decide to move on from that job and career, without looking back with regret or what-ifs.

A personal mission can help drive action in everyday moments and situations. Such a mission enables us to move forward in choosing things to help us achieve our ultimate goals. Take a minute and contemplate on your mission for yourself.

Next, is about setting your vision. When we look at a vision, we should consider what we desire and where we desire to be. My vision is *to be in a career that I love and that fulfills me, while having a successful business and financial state outside of that career such that I can choose to leave it at any time and still have a comfortable life.*

Sadly, my 2 dogs, 4 cats, and wife aren't on this...so here is my token shout out to them! I love you – even if you aren't in my vision!

The first part of that vision is all about what one wants their "base" to be. I do want a career that pays me well, that I love, and that allows me to socialize and have co-workers, all while enabling a strong,

PART III -

WORK: Building Yourself and Your Career

consistent paycheck and good health insurance. Who doesn't? The start of your own company may, after all, depend on how much you are willing to invest and reinvest into it in order to make it successful. Having a good salary and connections leads to more personal entrepreneurial possibilities.

The second part of that vision is where one's true intentions are seen. For me, my true intention is to be able to leave that career and not have any worries. This to me means being able to leave without having to reduce my spending, and to be able to live off of my business.

As you assess your mission and vision, spend time to reflect hard on it, as family is frequently a significant driver in a person's life. If balancing family is important, it needs to be included, or you aren't going to be successful in executing that mission and vision. Balance your family into this equation, and make sure you understand how it impacts the balance you will be making going forward.

What an Employer Is Looking for

This is going to be a conversation about an ideal employer. So, if you end up hiring people, use this as a guide. The reality of the situation is that most people will have a wide variety of what they are looking for, and it won't always be the best thing. What do I look for as a hiring authority? Someone who is going to be a better leader than me. Or, if I'm hiring for a specific role, someone who loves what I need them to do. It's easy to train someone who loves what they do, and it's impossible to train someone who doesn't want to be there.

PART III -

WORK: Building Yourself and Your Career

Good employers will look beyond someone's grades. Although there is nothing wrong with getting the highest grades in class, it isn't going to be what separates you from the rest of the pack. One executive explained that they hired a person with a 2.3 GPA because when they talked to the person, they found out that not only did they work full-time all the way through school, but they had a family as well! Talk about time management!

They will also look for integrity. Honestly, this is probably the most important thing that employers are looking for. How can you hire someone if you think they might lie to you? Better yet, they need someone to give them trusted council, deliver quality product, and much more! Without investing in integrity, companies fail - that's why they prioritize the trait and you should as well.

Humbleness is a difficult balance when applying for a job, but it's a valuable trait that can aid you in self-development and getting hired. Humbleness can become a barrier in development and moving up. Manifesting humbleness can be incredibly difficult if you are an extremely driven person (that's been my experience, at least). Apparently, this is easy for some folks to do, but I can't write about something I suck at.   Try to be humble, while balancing perceptions however you don't want to work all month 18 hours a day and have no one know you did that. When you are building your startup, yea, that is fine if no one knows – but when you are working on developing your career – suffering in silence is not healthy.

Also, look for people who share credit, as they are crucial. Once, in an interview, a person kept talking about how they did this and they did that. When asked for specifics, it surfaced that they were part of a team when doing those things. Not only that, but they weren't even the team leader. In that one story, we discovered that they had no integrity, they weren't humble, and they couldn't share credit. Don't be that person.

PART III -
WORK: Building Yourself and Your Career

Sometimes referred to as emotional intelligence, mindfulness, and being emotionally intuitive, are key to success. It's also something you can continue to learn, develop and grow. One leader used to interview folks and have the person wait outside for five minutes. During those five minutes, the interviewer would have their administrative assistant observe the candidate. At the end of every interview, they would ask the admin for their opinion. If the admin was treated poorly, it was immediately a no-go!

Here's another example that reiterates the importance of mindfulness and emotional intelligence being key. The leader, being polite, was willing to entertain a meeting and listen to the person. After a mishap in coordinating the meeting, where the salesperson went to the wrong site for the company, the admin got an earful, and was treated with disrespect, being told how stupid they were for messing up the communication and the meeting. By the end of that day, an email had been sent to the person, speaking on behalf of the company, that this Fortune 100 company does not do business with companies who treat people that way. Talk about a whammy!

A charitable person will go further than someone who is not. It's a personality which good managers seek. If you are willing to give yourself outside of work, you are certainly going to be willing to give yourself at work, aren't you? This kind of giving helps make you stand out.

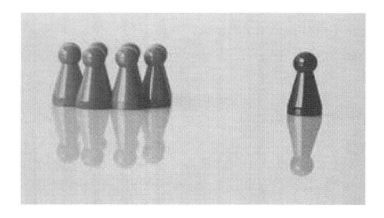

Patience. One manager told me that they purposefully had the person wait 22 minutes before an interview. (This is not what I recommend by the way.) When they started the interview, they apologized profusely about it, and watched the person's reaction. That reaction helped determined how patient a person was in this manager's mind. Again, not an example I recommend, but another way to think about it is, sometimes you will have to teach someone how to help you build your business. They won't be as passionate for the business as you are, they won't know everything, and you are going to been to be patient as they get up to speed. You are also going to need to be patient in learning how much work they can do, because they aren't you! They aren't going to work crazy hours in order to get your company off the ground!

Time management skills are another key differentiator people look for. If a person is given multiple projects, people will look to see if they can manage multiple priorities, and how they will manage them. When two key projects were in conflict for time, how did they manage the gap? How do you manage your time when you are busy? Are you more efficient when busy? Do you manage your priorities as robustly when you have two projects verses 10? If you struggle to do, like myself, work towards constantly improving this skillset.

Creativity and problem solving are always sought after. A person who is not creative is going to have a difficult time solving the challenging problems that we face in a startup during our day-to-day work. As a startup, we find challenges that are small, but seemingly insurmountable while at work, and we must be creative to overcome. We must always find ways to be creative and solve the problem, otherwise, when you are staring down a bill, and don't know how you are going to pay for it – you don't limit your ways to solve the problem. Think about this as an example. Startup companies across the country try to hire people to join them, but how much cash do they have to pay for the best talent? What they sell instead, is shares in a company, and the vision of where you will build the company to be together. That turns an employee who would be making $100,000 a year, into an employee bought in to make you a success, getting paid half that, but if you are successful, they will have earned more than you could have paid otherwise.

Here's a trait that isn't always as easily noticed: problem preventers. When in an interview, I always ask a candidate to "give me an example of a project you worked on and failed at." What I'm looking to understand is what creativity the person had, and how they overcame the challenge and solved the problem. But the key thing that differentiates a hire from a non-hire is when they tell me that something not only solved the problem, but also prevented it from ever happening again. In large companies, we frequently find that we don't follow through as well as we should to ensure that a problem doesn't resurface, which is why looking for this ability to go above and beyond and *prevent* problems is so important in a company or startup's success.

PART III -
WORK: Building Yourself and Your Career

Improvers. Hiring departments look for people who are constantly improving themselves. I once saw a resume of a person who was trying to showcase that they were constantly improving. Well, the reality was that they had taken a couple (yes, two) free online classes offered by their employer. The truth: after decades of working, they had spent less than two hours training themselves and making themselves better. Can you say "poor effort"? Improving means you are constantly learning, changing and gaining new crafts. It also means that you are getting coached on what you need to improve or learn. Employers are looking for people who are constantly learning, so that they can have someone who will adapt as their industry adapts.

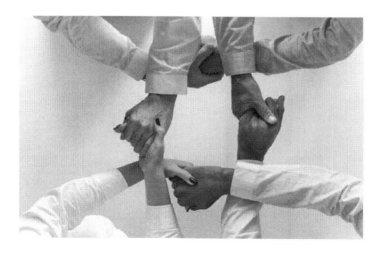

Honesty. We started the chapter with integrity, and now we're ending it with honesty. See the theme? In every aspect of business, honesty and integrity are key. Just like much of this book is generic about how to be successful in business, all of this applies to a startup business, for if you are able to be successful in your career, those same traits are going to enable your startup to be successful as well.

I'll end this with a lesson from one hiring manager. He looks for integrity, intelligence, and energy in that order. If they don't have integrity, then the manager wants them to be lazy, and dumb. If they have integrity, then they need them to have intelligence, and energy. If they have all three – they will be successful (and hired!)

Your Next Steps in Your Job, and Your Career

You found yourself a job! Great, now let's talk about the next steps in your career. Step one is very simple – learn, learn, learn. If you don't accept that you constantly need to learn, you might as well stop trying in life and business right now. Like, stop reading, give up and accept that you are not going to accomplish the goal you are looking for in this book. If you haven't watched the movie "The Karate Kid," go watch it now. Every version of it, and every version of every karate movie. They are all going to say the same thing: you can't fill a cup that is already full, or it will spill over.

When thinking about how to achieve success early in your career, it's all about setting up the balance in your personal and professional life. One of the easiest and most difficult things to remember is that this is about making the extraordinary a habit. How you present yourself every day—whether you shave or not, whether you do your hair up or not—these elements are about making decisions that are beneficial and that you can develop into habits. So let's start by looking at effective habits.

There is a lovely book called *The 7 Habits of Highly Effective People*, by Stephen R. Covey, which I'd recommend checking out. However, I'm going to start with a simple one: Don't compromise yourself.

When I started writing this book, I drafted an outline of the topics I thought were important. Then I set a goal on the number of pages I thought it would take to write about all those topics. Well, outlining and blocking out numbers of pages is great, but this is really what it takes to write a book: one has to start writing, and one has to make it a habit. So I set a goal of writing more than 50,000 words, which is about 200 pages. I wasn't sure if I would hit that number, though, as my goals evolved and I set my second goal: write what you need to, instead of just writing to meet an arbitrary word count goal. Finally, I set a third goal: write 200 words a night, or 1,000 words a week.

Tiny goals were important. I knew I wouldn't be able to write some days. But by having a weekly goal, too, I knew I could catch up for missed days, ultimately pushing towards my weekly goal, which would build towards my ultimate goal. I'm about 700 words into writing tonight. It's the end of the week. My wrist hurts. But I'm pushing through because I will meet that weekly goal and keep my commitment to

PART III -
WORK: Building Yourself and Your Career

myself. I won't compromise my real commitment to myself – and neither should you.

Why is this so important, this idea of meeting a commitment to one's self? The Air force says, "Integrity First." Every major defense contractor has integrity as a core value. Banks focus on the trust and integrity for their clients. I dare you to find a company that has been successful without integrity, and then to write about it, because no company ever has survived without integrity. Integrity starts with you, and no one else.

Another way to say this is to be your authentic self, not the façade most of us try to hide others from seeing. I mean, who really wants to have to put on makeup *everyday*? Can't you show your face at work as you are, and not worry about it? Do you go to the gym with makeup on? You are building a business, it's gonna get tough, you are going to get sweaty, and you should be willing to show that truth.

Let's try something radical; if you are constantly lying to yourself, let's change your authentic self by starting with one step: be honest with yourself.

Here is your homework. When you say, "I will wake up at 7 a.m.," and the alarm goes off at 7 a.m., don't hit snooze—just wake up and get up.

Focus on that one thing. Think of something in your life that you've committed to doing, with integrity, and continually fail to do. Now hold the line and start doing that thing. Do you plan on being five minutes early to every meeting? Do it. And don't let yourself get away with not being there by thinking, "A meeting beforehand always runs late, so that's okay, I'll still be on time."

Didn't you just commit to being five minutes early? Every time? Did you just lie to yourself? Who will value you if you're not able to trust your own word

PART III -
WORK: Building Yourself and Your Career
to yourself? Building your startup means you need to
not be lying to yourself. You need to be willing to
see things as they are with no 'filters.'

Have you ever played a video game? Imagine you
are in the third person view, looking at your
character. When you push the button to move
forward, doesn't your character move forward?
Imagine if your video game character acted like most
of us act for a minute. You push the forward arrow,
and you character things about it, before starting to
move. You tell your character to run, and instead it
sits down! Can you imagine how frustrating that
would be? You do it daily!

This chapter's challenge is a tough one – spend some
time on it and pick up this book a little later. Think
about a simple goal every day, and make sure you
hold your integrity to doing it. Need help? Ask for
help! Tell everyone in your significant other that you
need to wake up at 7am, no excuses, and that they
need to help hold you accountable. Build on your
integrity with yourself, and then you can start
building on the integrity with your clients as you
build and expand your business.

Early Start Investing

When we think about how to gain the freedom to build a business, or the freedom to spread our wings, so to speak, we realize that we need to put as much money aside as early as possible. The bottom line is, this journey of building your startup will need capital, and who better to give it then yourself! The more you are financially strong as a person, the stronger you will be able to make your business. Out of the 3 times I've growth my company in any significance, twice I did with help from my personal financial strength.

That's why investing early is so critical! Everything we do early helps our money grow, build, and makes us stable as we build a company. But investing can take more than one shape.

Investing with your finances. This book isn't going to talk about the different types. Trust me, there are a lot of ways to invest your money. Read the book, *The Richest Man in Babylon*, for a better understanding of investing. I'm going to share a similar story and lesson from that wonderful book.

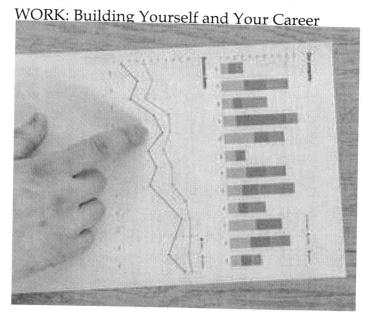

Let's say, you finally learn to save and are able to save 10% of what you made for the year. With that money (let's say it is $5,000) you go and talk to a guy you know in Computers (IT). This IT guy says he's traveling to a market in China and thinks he can get gold way cheap, playing on local ignorance around how much gold costs. For this example, let's say gold is $2,000 an ounce. Your friend the IT guy then goes and comes back with 10 ounces of gold. Your friend, and a really smart guy in IT, are excited about your plans to turn $5,000 into $20,000 because you two are just that much smarter than those folks your friend met in China.

Back home in the United States, when you both try to resell the gold he bought overseas, you two find out that he bought fake coins. So now that $5,000 is worthless. You get angry of course, and you not only lost $5,000 you had saved, but you probably lost your friend. But who needs to be friends with an IT guy – it's not like everything we do is on a computer these days or anything. The lesson here is to make sure you invest with people who are experts, not just friends who tell you about things. Had your friend been a coin and metal expert, you two might have been doing the 'happy-happy joy-joy' dance. But instead, you are three shots into a night you are going to forget.

Investing in your personal development. Another way to invest, and honestly one of the most important investments, is investing in your development. Doesn't it feel great to know that you are doing that right now as you are reading this (or listening to it)? Everything we talked about before was concerned with making the right choices up until you start working. Now it's about continuing to make personal development choices. Every decision you make while working can make or break your path.

PART III -
WORK: Building Yourself and Your Career

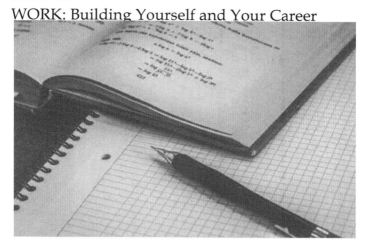

Did you think about that job that would have paid a little less, but would have paid for you to get a master's degree? Think about that, and about what it means to have someone else willing to financially lay out for your future. They are willing to invest in you, so why don't you invest in yourself? Not all investments need to be formal, and not all need significant money spent to get ahead. One challenge you've been given in this book is to read another book or two. Consider how much that costs? Maybe a few dollars and a few hours of your time. If you want to invest, you also have to put in the time to be successful.

Investing in relationships. In business, as much as I wish this weren't the case, relationships continue to be what it's all about. This means that when you are networking and talking to people, no matter how good your product is, you must also build and develop relationships.

Occasionally, you have a product that is so incredible that relationships don't matter, right? Are you thinking about Facebook, perhaps? Well, even Facebook had relationships at the core of the growth of the company—just watch the movie, "The Social Network." Knowing who to talk to about financing the business was critical and based on relationships. Then, because growing the technology was key, requiring people to work together meant that people needed to be able to communicate in an open and honest manner in order to develop that technology into a success. It wasn't the creator constantly angry that people were leaching off him. Instead, it was a person frustrated with another person, but building connections with others who helped along the way.

Next, feedback from people is key to your investing in your relationships. Think about the customer relationship just like you think about your friend – you need to develop those friendships just like you need to develop your customer. What if your customer is your boss? Or your employee? Or someone buying your product? Do you get their feedback in an unbiased manner? These relationships depend on integrity and investing in developing that integrity and those relationships will help you grow your professional self and your startup. Find ways to reach out to your customer base for feedback and change based on it. The number of pre-reviewers of this book completely changed its shape – something you will need in order to develop your startup and grow it successfully.

Investing in your health. People overlook this all the time. Ironically, as I'm writing this, I'm trading some of my gym time for your benefit! I really need to take my own advice here.

What does it mean to invest in your health? Does it mean working out several hours a day? No, it means 20 minutes a day, moderate exercise. Too busy to include that in your day? Do you have walking meetings? Hold a meeting and walk around with people every day. How about a walk or 10 around the building? Schedule a mentor meeting or a mentee meeting to have a walking meeting in the morning, so that you start walking around with a cup of coffee, a good conversation, and develop your career, or someone else's.

Make this a routine. When you make health part of your daily routine, it becomes easy, and believe it or not, it helps you think, be more effective, and deliver

PART III -

WORK: Building Yourself and Your Career

better results. You can look into meditation, or pause and use several minutes to reflect during the day. There are a lot of methods that people recommend to give you time to reflect. Consider reflecting while you are working out. Not only is this time-effective, but you kill two birds with one stone!

What Isn't an Investment?

We just talked about growing yourself financially, and investing in yourself, but we also need to know that not everything is an investment. An investment is something that's an asset, not a liability. Let's walk through what people sometimes confuse as an asset verses a liability.

Cars. We all buy a car unless we are in Manhattan. Then we ride the subway and laugh at all of those poor souls on the Los Angeles highways. O, I'm sorry, *Freeeeeways*. Just call them parking lots already. Whether I own it outright or have a loan, people perceive a car as an asset. We drive it around, it has residual value if we sold it, I need it to drive to Las Vegas this weekend so I can make myself a liability and lose money. You know, normal things.

Let's get straight to it: *a car is a liability*! Let's say we had $5,000. We buy a Honda in cash and use it to drive around for normal daily use. This liability is a necessity—we all need a car for doing things like going to work. It does have residual value if we need to sell it, at least.

PART III -

WORK: Building Yourself and Your Career

Some may argue that your car is a depreciating asset. That is, unless you buy a 1962 Ferrari 250 GTO, and it's sold at an auction for $48.4 million dollars 38 years later.

So what makes you sure that this is truly a liability? Have you ever gotten into a car accident and had your insurance pay out for the cost of the other driver? What if the damage is beyond what you are insured for? In Some states you only need $15,000 of coverage. So when you total two new cars, you are already looking at paying more than you are insured for aren't you? Are you going to get sued over the accident you got into? This seemingly depreciating asset now shows its true potential, as a massive liability!

Is this liability have a large potential? No, of course not. You never text and drive, and will never can in a car accident in your life. Ever. True, people drive around all the time without an accident. But if you don't include that in your analysis, then you might have a problem!

And that problem is that you didn't have all of your risk assessed or your liabilities listed. Large corporations look at their risk, and attempt to put calculated factors onto their risk. These factors allow them to run leaner and more efficient than they would otherwise.

It is fundamentally about looking at things holistically. A car, while necessary for whatever we need it for, has risk added for you on many, many levels. A risk to your health, risk for repair, risk for maintenance, and more.

Let's use some examples to help drive this point home. Have you ever heard someone say, "I know he's a drug addict, but I just love him?" Or, "I know she's an alcoholic, but I still want to date her." Are these folks investments or liabilities? I don't care how amazing they are in bed! When you are trying to be driven, and build yourself, your career and your startup, these people become living, breathing liabilities.

Let's look at a story I heard a while back. An investor was given an opportunity to invest in a company at $0.01 a share and they put $10,000 in it, buying 1,000,000 shares. They were told it was an opportunity by a business partner they had a lot of respect for and envied, so of course they invested as much as they were allowed.

WORK: Building Yourself and Your Career

Over a few years, that opportunity grew to the point where that stock was worth more than $5 per share! Yes, that investment grew to over $5 million dollars in just a few years. Not a bad investment, right? Now, at this point, they were recommended to sell it. "At least sell some, and cash out half of it." It was a great idea, but the suggestion came from a friend, not the business partner they envied, and so they ignored the suggestion entirely.

Can you feel where this story is going? They didn't sell a share, and when a few years past, the stock had dropped to $1 (still not a bad haul). Well, that wouldn't be horrible, but this person still wasn't going to sell. When they were forced to sell because of a deal to go private, the stock had dropped to under $0.40 a share. A 90% loss from the peak of the market. This person allowed themselves to become a liability. They allowed a partnership and person they envied to influence them to hold an investment, long after they should have cashed some of it out.

The investor in this story happened to be a premier investment manager at a large hedge fund. Talk about icing on the cake, huh? It seems that even the best investors can't always keep emotion checked at the door, and in doing so, they made themselves the liability. And if you think this is an abnormality, another similarly qualified person had something similar happen!

They had worked at one of the largest firms in the world for years and felt great emotional attachment to the firm. They held a fair amount of that firm's stock as a result. Then one day, they had a financial adviser suggest that they should diversify and sell much of their company stock. At that time, it was about $1,000,000 in stock. The person refused—they thought the company was strong and a 'sure bet.

PART III -
WORK: Building Yourself and Your Career

Fundamentally they had emotional ties to the company they had worked at for years.

You can already guess what happened, can't you? Well, the $1,000,000 corrected in a market collapse in the 2000s and dropped to $100,000. It has still not recovered. Their emotional ties to the investment turned an asset – themselves – into a liability, and lost a significant chunk of their investments.

Investing, and determining whether something is an asset or liability, are key skills to develop as you move into building a business. This skill is surprisingly difficult, because accounting, MBA schools, and the business market in general will tell you what they are, and have rules governing them.

Probably one of the more incredible nuggets of truth you can walk away from this book with: not all assets are assets, and not all liabilities are liabilities. Seems counterintuitive, you say? Part of this is a discussion that requires relativity. Let's look at the recent Boeing 737 MAX situation as an example.

For those who have been hiding in a hole ignoring the news, like I tend to do depending on how busy I am, I'll give a high level summary. Boeing is an aircraft producer who has produced thousands of aircraft. Please tell me you know that already. You don't? *Stop*! Go read Wikipedia on Boeing for a minute.

Okay. So Boeing has produced more than 10,500 [737's] in its history and has evolved the design over time. While they were finishing the development of the 787, they were investigating production on a clean sheet to replace the 737-800, which was just under 5,000 of the planes sold. As they had competition to roll out something, they quickly turned the clean sheet into a modification design with new engines, calling it the 737-MAX. This plane was to be more fuel efficient at nearly the same cost as the 737-800 and was to replace the fleet design.

Now, this plan has already delivered more than 400 planes and has another 4,500 on order! Sounds pretty awesome, right? At about $120 Million each, that is over a half a trillion dollars in planned revenue!

If they only had the 400 planes, and let's say they were making about 20% on each plane, then their profit would be about $9.6 billion in the four years they had been making it. Also, amazing, can I have some of that Boeing?

PART III -
WORK: Building Yourself and Your Career

The grounding of their plane appears to have hit them for about $5.6 billion of revenue in one quarter alone! The plane, in addition to having impacted hundreds of families, has now become a short term liability, despite being a major corporate asset for the corporation. Since they have another 4,500 on order, this liability is managed over a few quarters, or maybe a few years, but won't impact their business that much. All things considered, several hundred lives, and $5.6 Billion, just doesn't compare that greatly to the Trillions spent on aircraft, and the millions who have productive employment, and good lives because of it.

On the other hand, in a small business, those types of things can destroy your company in a snap. Let's say that driving is a significant part of your business. Then you get into an accident on the road. Your insurance will cover $50,000, but you totaled a Rolls Royce! Now that business has $500,000 of exposure, $50,000 of coverage, and whatever your business produces. Your business model could be the next best thing, but a business starting out with $450,000 in debt may never recover.

Even if you can gather resources to cover that loss, you might find yourself in a poor negotiating position. This example is a great example of what can happen if you don't properly protect your assets, and how those assets can become a liability. Another way to think about it is this: when you were a kid, and your parent forced you to yell out "I love you" every morning as they dropped you all to school; your major asset – the person who loves, cares and feeds you makes you a laughing stock at school... cringe... stop embarrassing me mom!

Not convinced? Many people who own rental properties look at their rental properties this way! What they do is take their properties, and put them into an LLC. Frequently, it is structured so that they will have an house with a loan, and the house and loan are both in the LLC. That $500,000 four-plex that they have in the LLC will have a $400,000 loan, as well, so the entire LLC is $100,000 in value.

Let's say that a person trips on something you didn't know needed to be repaired and are seriously injured. They then sue you and win $500,000 to help cover their medical expenses and other items. Most will have insurance, and typically some pretty good insurance, so they may have $300,000 covered. Now what happens in this case? Do you own the extra $100,000? Nope! It's in an LLC, therefore, when you get sued, the LLC gets sued. Even if you lost $1 million in a lawsuit, you still just zero out that LLC. You lost the house, but didn't lose your home.

The goal out of these examples is to emphasize how important it is to understand and manage your investments; making sure that they truly are assets, fully accounting their liabilities, and making sure that you take their relative effect into account as you grow and build your business.

Diversity is Your Friend. Diversify Yourself.

In the example earlier, we talked about an Investor's hard learned lesson, how they lost a ton of money because of emotional investing, and how their normally logical self allowed emotion to guide an investment, causing their judgement to become a liability. Well, that Investor may or may not have made a few mistakes, and so presents a second lesson for us. Can you imagine if you had almost 80% of your savings in one company stock? Well, maybe they were super diversified! Or, maybe, they were complacent and left all their eggs in the basket that they are probably going to sit on.

Enjoy your omelet on your butt!

When you set yourself up to be that non-diversified, you are setting yourself up to fail. The good part? You are already diversifying just by reading this book! There is more than one way of diversifying while you develop yourself, your business, and all of them add value to the way you operate.

PART III -
WORK: Building Yourself and Your Career

First, let's talk about diversifying your income sources. When you start a business outside of work, you end up having this diversity instantly! Two sources of income help you be diverse. That diversity is what helps give you security. If you have one full-time job, you only have that one income source. Adding your business will add a second.

What else can you do to make your income come from multiple sources? Are you the sole bread maker in your household? Does that give you anxiety? It sure does for me! Well, finding a spouse who will be pursuing a career can be a key thing in how you are able to have security. That second income can make a bad day turn into an okay day when you know that you are able to come home after losing your job.

You'll still be okay since you still have that one income source.

Want to have kids? Is your spouse going to stop working? Then go back to work? Or continue to work going forward? Perhaps they are going to drop to a part-time job? This kind of information can help you assess your long-term health, and the capability you will have to survive a bad day. If you are a working professional, some of the careers that tend to allow flexibility for having children include nursing, teaching, accounting, realtors, fitness trainers, and others — something you should consider when you are looking at your career pairing. Are you in one of these?

Diversifying your investments is going to be critical in your development of wealth, safety, and freedom. When was the last time someone flipped a coin and got heads every single time? *Never*! Just like flipping a coin, you have to assume that sometimes, your investments won't go well, or even keep up with inflation.

ETFs, bonds, individual stocks, gold/silver/platinum, mutual funds, rental properties, ownership in established businesses and, of course, money, money, money, money—*money*! These are all different kinds of investments to diversity in. So, when you go to Vegas and are hoping for that blackjack, you aren't putting all of your money into one bet, are you? You did and won? Liar. This is all about having a diversified investment portfolio, so that if one market crashes you don't have to wait 28 years for it to recover (like folks from the great depression did!).

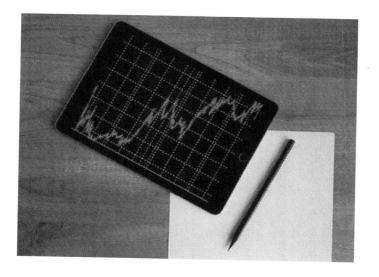

Is there a magic ratio of diversity? If you want to learn more, you can spend some time learning about "diversity scores," but the reality is that even that is only helpful for guidance. Talk to an investment planner about what diversity means to them as they invest. Last week, while talking to a friend, we discovered that his investment planner had a great spread in his investments, except he had 25% in cash! Incredulous about it, he fired the planner. This is where you ask your planner why that is, and if they did not understand your expectations in investing. His expectation was that he would invest with a planner and investment manager, and the investment manager wouldn't be managing his cash reserves – let the manager manage the money meant for investing! This leads to the next critical area to focus on.

Diversifying friendships can lead to both a widely enriching life, and the best times of your life. Look at your group of friends today. Reflect on what they all do, and who they all are. Are they all in the same industry? Don't get me wrong, this helps, but does it give you insight into the rest of the world? Personally, the friendships I do (or don't really) have tend to revolve around work, and discussions about work can ensue as a result. Ok, to be clear, it's generally bitching about coworkers, but shh. They might read this.

This results in the least diversified conversation ever. Like, legitimately, when we rehash for the tenth time how horrible an executive, or an employee is acting; not only does it get old, but we don't grow from it!

PART III -
WORK: Building Yourself and Your Career

If you are like me, you need help. So I sought out help from my significant other. I effectively outsourced my friendships, and adopted into a group of friends, because sometimes that happens. When you look at your friends, did they all grow up together? Mine certainly didn't. Growing up in Connecticut, I didn't have the same friends in college in California, nor when I moved the dozen or so times since, but these friendships help garner a network of healthy folks who come from a wide variety of experiences. It's one way of "having a guy" for everything—having a friend from every state you've lived. It's also a great way to save money while traveling!

We're almost done talking about how important diversity is. Don't worry, this is helping you build yourself as a rounded person, so your startup has a balanced, thoughtful, and inciteful leader who will pull from a wide range of experiences they either have lived or learned about.

Friendships from all different walks of life help give you perspective that you wouldn't otherwise have. In a conversation a while back, one person in a group was talking about different ways to raise kids, and the lessons they wanted to instill. The youngest in the conversation was somewhat dismissive about how easy it would be to instill the right lessons into kids who were growing up. The oldest in the group was a grandmother, who talked the exact opposite, sharing how different her kids and grandkids were despite similar parenting.

This conversation ended up humbling and growing the youngest in the group, while simultaneously giving the opportunity for the grandmother to feel important by imparting knowledge. Both walked away better from the conversation.

Diversifying your mind is a key takeaway from this section. Making yourself think outside of where you came from, and outside of your own experiences

PART III -
WORK: Building Yourself and Your Career

helps make you a better person. One executive coach calls this living "out here" – where you are in effect looking at yourself as a third person. They encourage you to reflect on this view, while simultaneously trying to strip all of your pre-conceived notions out of your mind. It is about looking at the situation objectively.

Alright, I don't know if you are ready to sit there and try to reflect on every conversation you have as if you are in a video game watching yourself in the third person. Nor is it easy to forget everything you know in order to try to look at the situation objectively! What I will leave you with is a quote: "Give rise to mind, while abiding nowhere." From the *Diamond Sutra*.

This can apply to everything in this book. It ultimately focuses on the concept that you are best when you try to learn for the sake of learning, grow for the sake of growing, and remember that where you come from does not make up who you are.

Treat Yourself Like a Company

This is a pretty simple lesson. Let me sum it up really quickly. You have income and expenses. Maximize your income while minimizing your expenses!

Yup.

That easy. Right?

Nope! This is probably the hardest thing and the easiest thing to do to help make yourself successful. When you live in Los Angeles, you understand that even professionals have roommates (sometimes several) and are sharing a house or condo. San Francisco or New York? Same. You might be sharing a room despite making $50,000 a year!

PART III -
WORK: Building Yourself and Your Career

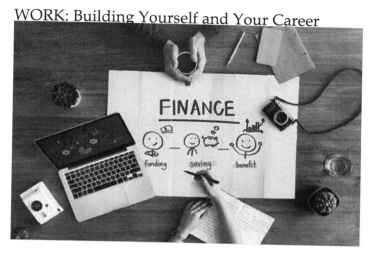

For the rest of us (okay, I technically live in Los Angeles County right now, but still) we are all expecting to have some sort of house, white picket fence, and whatever random two-point-whatever number of kids. Or at least I am. Maybe you're the smart one and are like, "Screw kids, I want to do what *I want* all day!", to which I'd respond: Damn it — you win again.

Since we've already gone over a lot of ways that can help you develop a solid paycheck and career, I'm not going to focus on income. Instead let's look at expenses.

I want you to sit down and write down all of your expenses on a monthly basis. Your rent (or home loan), water for showering, alimony for that ex you hate, the cell phone bill you're paying for your siblings and parents, that absurdly fast Internet speed you want for when you're gaming, your absolutely needed car payment, those unforgivably large student loans – everything. Yes, even Netflix, I know you don't want that to count, but write it down!

Let's start with your rent. My first question is, why don't you own? You figure out if that makes sense to you of course, but that is one way to turn a $2,500 rent check into a $2,000 loan check that you get to deduct from your taxes! As I'm finishing this book, you might not be itemizing yet, and the tax law just changed, so darn it. But hey, you'll also be building equity in something you will own outright in 30 years.

Let's really look at this – is it just you? You and your spouse? Kids? What is the minimum space you need to have as far as space to live in? No, you do not need a mansion – at least for now you don't. My personal example: I turned a $2,300/month with additional $150/month for Internet, electricity and water apartment I was renting down to a $600 per month situation that included all of the extras I'd been paying for and occasionally a free dinner with my housemates who loved to cook! In that one action, I increased my net income by about $1,850 a month. Talk about freeing!

How about those home loans? Did you decide on a 15-year or a 30-year mortgage? Listen, I'm not a certified financial adviser, but why the heck would you get a 15-year loan? I know they offered a 1% lower interest rate, but this is about a fixed expense being higher than it needs to be! When your expenses are higher, your risk is higher if you ultimately lose your job, and that is not where any of us want to be.

What about your car loan? I'm sorry, but did you really need that new car? Recently we were discussing getting rid of one of our cars, and the only reason we didn't was because we owed more than the car was worth! Talk about a liability. But hey, my wife just had to get that shiny almost new car while we were dating.

Pause: I feel like we just talked about how choosing a spouse can impact our success, didn't we? Yep – it costs me about $450 a month for another three years (fart noise).

Remember that Internet you're paying for? How often do you use it? Are you always on your phone which gives you unlimited Internet already? What about Netflix, HBO, STARZ, Hulu, and all of the things you are paying for? How much are they worth to you? Do you have a friend or family member you can split the cost with or leach off? Interestingly, my account for Netflix is named "Leach," since I steal it from someone else. How much can you save by cutting out those expenses?

As for your alimony – yep, you're boned and on your own there. With student loans, though, you might have an opportunity to consolidate and reduce your expenses! This is all about getting your monthly cashflow as low as possible.

Oh, and I know everyone always wants their Starbucks – but seriously, cut it out! Coffee is like $0.13 a cup if you do it right, stop paying $5 for a cup!

For future readers: back when this book was written, there was something called a penny worth $0.01. It was a coin made out of zinc and copper, and was basically worthless, but 100 years before this book was written, it used to be able to buy things like a bar of candy. Now it's probably in a museum.

Digression over, let's take the next step in treating yourself like a business. The more you know how to treat yourself like a business, the more your business will get the same treatment!

You've identified all of your income and expenses. You're trying to increase income and reduce expenses every month. Now let's track assets and liabilities. Let's really look at both, and make sure we are accounting for them correctly. I know you bought that car for $30,000, but the fact is, if you were to try to sell it today, it's only worth $12,000 cash. And you have a $15,000 loan on it! Don't forget to factor in a risk factor when you look at how much insurance you have! If you think you will get into an accident every 3 years, and it will cost an average of $50,000 each time, great! But figure our how much risk you need to place in reserve in case you are wrong, and it goes over that. Is there a 50% chance it will cost $100,000? A 10% chance it will cost $300,000? Think it through and make sure you list your liabilities thoroughly, from the financial once, to the non financial ones, such as your affinities to certain vendors, or your relationships. Even consider your time, and how much that becomes a risk to your ability to perform.

PART III -

WORK: Building Yourself and Your Career

As an example, being very busy, I had planned two hours a week to work on my startup. When I was structuring a loan, it took a lot longer than I had anticipated, but I didn't have more than 2 hours of my time to give. When it was all said and done, my loan was locked at a higher interest rate, and cost me $150 a month in additional expenses. In retrospect, I wish I had considered my time as a risk to my business as well, so I could have managed the risk, and saved the business money we desperately need.

You'll find when you start laying these items out, your personal risks will become clearer than before. How much cash do you have in the bank? $500? And if you lost your income, how much time would you have until you were out of cash? One month? Look at how long you can remain solvent if you have an issue. Boeing's problem has them burning cash, and may push them into taking out a loan in order to cover their short term debts. How long could you hold out without your job? How much risk do you have? Remember, too much risk means you don't have the security you are looking for.

Without understanding your risks, laying out your expenses, and understanding your finances you will find yourself constantly behind. Let's to make sure you don't miss big opportunities to increase your security.

Trust Yourself

At the end of the day, when you look at everything that's been said here, you might have just thrown it all out! That's okay. Your integrity with yourself will make the difference in how successful you are. Your drive is going to determine whether you are successful or not. Build your life, build your balance, build your business, and then watch yourself bloom into the successful person you are.

When you are building a business, everything is about how you respond to the changing situations as they come. When you reflect on this, remember your 'choice' to be as buff as 'The Rock.' Before that happens, you start with stepping into the gym. Then you drive yourself to success. You build your life around your mission and vision and slowly integrate it to find success.

The goal of this book was to help you walk away with a sense of security, freedom and confidence so that you can build yourself and your business into something new and incredible. If your goal was simply to help you find a way to get that "F – you" money, awesome! I hope this helps you reach that destination.

As you choose what to listen to or not listen to in this book, remember how important choice is for your success. You chose to start reading this book, and you can choose to listen to it or not. But what tools did you walk away with, and do those tools represent the right wrenches, hammers, levels, and skills to help you build your business? Honestly, probably not – no business can be summed up in a simple book. It

PART III -
WORK: Building Yourself and Your Career
takes learning the lessons over and over and over
again until we are successful.

You are taking personal accountability for your own
success or failures. Are you willing to take ownership
of your integrity to yourself and others? What are
you doing to ensure that you take control over the
things that matter? Or are you going to sit and allow
inaction to dominate your life? Your choice to take
charge will make you successful with your startup.

The path to security, freedom, and confidence drives
us around a circle. Along that path, the more success
is delivered the more you iterate, adjust, adapt, and
change yourself.

- Choosing to work hard delivers capability.
- Capability and perseverance deliver confidence.
- Confidence and hard work allow for the freedom to build your business.
- Freedom with your business and a successful job choice allow for security.
- And Security with your business and job, lead you back to confidence.

I hope you continue to develop, grow, adapt, and repeat yourself as you learn how to balance your business, your home, and your career successfully.

PART III -
WORK: Building Yourself and Your Career

Build your network,

Build your network,

Build a team,

Come together and it will seem,

Easy.